DISCERNING YOUR VOCATION

THE PAULINE FAMILY

Visit our web site at
www.stpauls.us

or call 1-800-343-2522
and request current catalog

Discerning Your Vocation
A Catholic Guide for Young Adults

Fr. Nathanael Pujos
Fr. Anthony Ariniello
Sr. Emmanuelle Borchardt
of the
COMMUNITY OF THE BEATITUDES

Preface by Father Jacques Philippe

ST PAULS

Library of Congress Cataloging-in-Publication Data

Ariniello, Anthony.
  Discerning your vocation: a Catholic guide for young adults / Fr. Anthony Ariniello,
Sr. Emmanuelle Borchardt, and Fr. Nathanael Pujos / preface by Father Jacques
Philippe.
     pages cm.
  ISBN 978-0-8189-1373-0
1. Work—Religious aspects—Catholic Church. 2. Vocation—Catholic Church. I. Title.
  BX1795.W67A75 2014
  261.8'5—dc23
                              2014016035

Produced and designed in the United States of America by the
Fathers and Brothers of the Society of St. Paul,
2187 Victory Boulevard, Staten Island, New York 10314-6603
as part of their communications apostolate.

ISBN 978-0-8189-1373-0

Current Printing - first digit   1   2   3   4   5   6   7   8   9   1 0

Place of Publication:
2187 Victory Blvd., Staten Island, NY 10314 - USA

Year of Current Printing - first year shown

2014   2015   2016   2017   2018   2019   2020   2021   2022   2023

Table of Contents

✝ *It is Jesus in fact that you seek when you dream of happiness;*
he is waiting for you when nothing else you find satisfies you;
he is the beauty to which you are so attracted;
it is he who provokes you with that thirst for fullness
that will not let you settle for compromise;
it is he who urges you to shed the masks of a false life;
it is he who reads in your hearts your most genuine choices,
the choices that others try to stifle.
It is Jesus who stirs in you the desire to do
something great with your lives,
the will to follow an ideal, the refusal to allow yourselves to be
grounded down by mediocrity,
the courage to commit yourselves humbly and patiently to
improving yourselves and society,
making the world more human and more fraternal.

Pope John Paul II,
World Youth Day 2000 (Tor Vergata-Rome)

Preface

Fr. Jacques Philippe, CB

I recently read a text from Saint Edith Stein (otherwise known as Sr. Teresa Benedicta of the Cross, a Jewish convert who died in Auschwitz). She was speaking of the period of her life after becoming Catholic but before entering the Carmelites. Having been asked to give conferences on various topics, she affirmed that, in the end, she only had one "small and simple truth" that she wanted to communicate: how wonderful to walk along in life "holding the hand of the Lord."

I am moved by this same conviction: the most beautiful thing in this world is to be led by the hand of God. Not going at it alone when we pursue our interests and goals, but rather taking it on together with Someone who knows and loves us. Not building my life alone, but in a loving and trusting communion with God, the One who knows us better than we know ourselves, who created us with infinite tenderness, and who knows which path will lead us to happiness and fruitfulness. Someone who understands our weaknesses and limits, who knows us as we are, and who infinitely respects our freedom, more than anyone else we could find. To be led like a child grasping his father's hand, a Father who loves each person in a special way and has a unique vocation for everyone. The call may not always be easy to understand or to follow, but it is an inexhaustible source of joy and fruitfulness.

This book by the Community of the Beatitudes embodies this desire. Addressed to students and young adults who are in search of God's will, it presents the conditions and lifestyle which help to promote a personal relationship with the Lord, and to let oneself be taken by the gentle hand of the Father. It outlines elements of good discernment as well as traps to avoid in order to discover and put into practice the call He addresses to each person.

I hope that it encourages many young people to be open to God's call for their life, giving them the necessary light to understand it and then freely respond. May they have the grace to discover the unique place they have in the mystery of the Church, the role they can play in the coming of the Kingdom, and the joy they can share with the Virgin Mary as she proclaims: "The Almighty has done great things for me, and holy is his Name!"

Introduction

For I know well the plans I have in mind
for you, says the Lord,
plans for your welfare, not for woe!
Plans to give you a future full of hope.

(Jeremiah 29:11)

This is a short book compared to the fundamental questions it will address: What does God expect from me? What does He want for my life? What is my vocation? Where can I find my true happiness on this earth? More specifically: What should be my state of life? How do I know if I am called to be a priest? Or what about a religious sister? Should I get married and start a family? Is this person "the one," the soul that is destined to become my "better half"?

One may tremble, and rightly so at having to face such deep questions. But at the same time, we put our trust in God, who is a Father who promises to bring about the good future we hope for. His peace awaits us at the end of every valley of darkness. His promises triumph over every uncertainty, every doubt, and every suffering.

The answer to the vocation question is an intimate matter, between you and the Lord. What we can humbly offer are some clear principles to help you navigate your discernment along the right path. The advice is concrete, while the tone is light and sometimes funny. Isn't God eternal joy?

Before setting out to be a priest, consecrated or married, remember that there is an even deeper question: What type of holiness does the Lord want for me? Everyone is called to be a saint: single people, married people, religious, and priests. What kind of saint is the Lord calling me to be? In the end, holiness is the only thing that counts. It is the universal vocation, applicable to everyone. At the end of our lives, God will not ask us if we were consecrated, priests or married! He will only

ask us, "Have you loved?" As doctor of the Church, St. John
of the Cross, said, "In the evening of life, we will be judged on
love alone." The question of our particular vocation can thus
be rephrased: For you, which path will allow you to love better
and to give yourself to God and others: is it by raising a family,
by being a priest, by being a religious brother or sister, or living
out a vocation of single life? Your state of life (celibate, married, priest) is important, but remember that it is only a *path*
to holiness, not the goal itself. It is a means – the field, if you
like – where your sanctification takes place. Deeply engraved
in each of us lies our primary call to holiness, and all vocations
are at the service of this call. To become a saint is exactly what
God expects from you! ★

This reminder is important for you at the beginning of
this book. It puts things into perspective, taking a step back in
order to begin this path peacefully, without any pressure. Many
young adults who remain single may feel that they are single
"by default," not yet having found the right match or frustrated
by situations that did not work out. This is not necessarily the
case, and we will address why. Life is not wasted or lost if you
fail to find a soul mate or the right community! Without the
"prestige" of a religious order or the priesthood, or without the
"security" of a family, your vocation remains exactly the same:
holiness and love. Furthermore, your infinite dignity as a son or
daughter of God endures, as does the unconditional love and
tenderness God has for you.

The structure of the book is simple: first, it will seek to
help *ground* the discernment (Part I), then go over the criteria
of the *discernment process* (Part II), then *protect* it from some

common pitfalls (Part III), and finally *carry it out* (Part IV).
Before reading any further, take a moment to pray: entrust yourself to God at the beginning of this book, to His Holy Spirit, and ask Him to reveal how He will make your life a victory and a blessing. If you have this book in your hands, it is because you are asking yourself about your call, and so the Lord's grace must already be at work in your heart. So let us take a moment to thank Him, before even embarking on our journey.

I

Grounding Discernment with
Good Foundations

If you have a sporting event coming up, you take time to train. You get tips from your coach and teammates; you avoid alcohol, cigarettes or junk food. You examine the court or field, double check your equipment, scout your opponent and devise strategies, and verify the playing conditions. In short, you prepare everything to maximize your chances of victory.

When writing a term paper for a class, the procedure is the same. What type of paper is it? Which topic would meet the teacher's expectations? How many pages should it be? What guidelines are given? Where can appropriate sources be found? Who might have good advice? How can you be effective in your research, moving quickly and without wasting time?

In school and sports, preparation is 90% of the work.

In the same way, you can prepare the way for the Lord's call to come into your life. You have met God, and you know that He is madly in love with you. You want to love Him too. But how? Listen to your heart? Even there, seemingly contradictory signs can appear. Fortunately there are some solid guidelines that will help you make your choice, to cooperate with the Lord's grace in a prudent and peaceful way. Four principles, outlined in this chapter, can help lay the groundwork for proper discernment.

There is just one prerequisite: peace. Peace is not simply the goal that you will reach only at the end of your journey, once you know for sure "what God wants for you" (a questionable expression, as you will see). Rather, peace of heart is already important at the start of the journey. This puts things in perspective, so that the discernment will not overwhelm you. You must not stress out about it to the point of losing sleep or getting sick.

The fundamental attitude of the heart is one of surrender to God. It is important that before beginning the four steps of this chapter, you have already found peace. This peace and deep joy are two fruits of the Spirit that can be experienced immediately. They testify that your life is already surrendered to the Father in a filial relationship consisting of trust and faith, with the certitude that nothing can separate you from His Love, no matter what happens. He has written your name in the palm of His hand, and whatever happens, He will always bless you.

1. A prayer life in 4G!

In order to know if someone is the love of your life, you first have to meet him or her, spend time together, talking and listening to each other. Otherwise, you risk falling in love in your head, making up romantic movies Hollywood-style, but not getting any closer to "the real thing." With God, it's the same. If you want to know Him, you have to spend time with Him, speak with Him, and listen to Him. This is called prayer. "Prayer means talking with God as a friend speaks to a friend," said St. Ignatius. God is the best of friends, since He knows us and loves us better than we know and love ourselves!

Here are four pillars, which are key to building a solid prayer life and communicating with God... in 4G! (Grab, Go, Gaze, Glorify).

• GRAB *your Bible every single day*

When someone you love lives far away, communication keeps the fire of love alive. What lover has not read the letter from his girlfriend twenty times? The Bible, the Gospel, is like a love letter that God wrote to you. It becomes "alive" for you if the God who wrote it lives in your heart, and if you know that He wrote it for you. This means you, personally. God does not love mankind in general, but He loves Mike, Jessica, Carmen and Daniel, each in a specific way. Thus, the reading of the Gospel will help you remember the love, alive and always present, with which you are loved in a unique and personal way. If you read the Bible every day, you will often be touched by this or that verse which will speak to exactly what you are going through and which will provide you with the answer you were seeking.

But for this to happen, you need to spend time reading the Gospel on a regular basis, letting it nourish you, copying the verses that touch you today, even learning them by heart. How often we waste time reading junk in the news, browsing Facebook posts and pictures, or embarking on a wild goose chase of "interesting" links on the Internet. Why not use this time for God instead?

Aim for one chapter of the Gospel per day, for starters.

• GO *to Mass and Confession*

These are two sacraments which you cannot do without, because they are like bread and water for your soul.

The bread is the Mass. It gives you a strength which is beyond you: God himself comes to you in the Eucharist, in a mysterious way. He strengthens your will, gives you courage to live and fight as a Christian, strengthens your mind, and gives you a maturity and clarity that others often lack. Finally, through the Eucharist, God wants to purify your desires and your passions, and constantly remind you that He loves you. Sunday Mass is not only mandatory – it is necessary. If you find some time to go during the week too, go for it! This is food for your soul.

The water is Confession. It is the water that purifies and washes. Sometimes we are like children who run away at bath time! And yet penitence is how our being is gradually purified. Regular confession prevents minor injuries from becoming infected; it helps you keep the pleasing fragrance of Christ. Your ears, well-cleaned, can recognize the voice of the Beloved from all the other voices that speak within you or around you. Going to Confession at least once a month is a good goal for a young adult who is discerning.

• GAZE at Jesus in the Blessed Sacrament

Adoration is a simple prayer. You are alone with your God, in a heart-to-heart with Jesus present in the host, in the Blessed Sacrament exposed on the altar or in the tabernacle. Many parishes and religious communities offer Adoration of the Blessed Sacrament. If you really cannot find an opportunity to benefit from the presence of Jesus in the Blessed Sacrament, you can have this "heart-to-heart" with God elsewhere. Go to a meditative place, since He is present everywhere – above all in your heart where the Holy Spirit dwells.

You can also pray in your room, taking Jesus' advice in

Matthew 6:6: "But when you pray, go into your room and shut the door and pray to your Father who is in secret; and your Father who sees in secret will reward you." Or you can pray while walking in nature. Any place where you feel at ease, and where you can speak freely with the Lord – even out loud – is appropriate for prayer. You can tell Him everything: nothing shocks God! He is a Father!

During adoration, you will remember what you may have forgotten: God is Love, and nothing but Love! That means that He will not judge you, He will not spy on you, and He will not ask you to be someone you are not. He loves you unconditionally, to the point of folly (that of the Cross, as St. Paul says), which means more than any person on this earth.

No one, not even yourself, can change His love for you or separate you from Him (Romans 8:38). It is difficult to realize this because it is the kind of love which we cannot find anywhere else. Indeed, the love of our parents can come close, but the majority of people around us love us as long as we behave a certain way. How many "friends" would stay your friend if you suddenly became unbearable to them? God's love, on the other hand, is unconditional. It will not change, even if you become hateful toward Him, even if you nail Him to the Cross. What changes when you sin is not His Love for you; rather it is your joy, because you forget how much you are precious and unique to your God. Think about Adam and Eve hiding in the garden, while God is calling out to them (Genesis 3:9). Think about the Prodigal Son (Luke 15): while the father remains there, waiting on the doorstep for his son's return, the son goes far away and is damaged greatly by his sin.

In adoration, you kneel there before God, a child under the proud gaze of your Father's unfathomable love. He looks into the deepest desires of your heart, those desires you have to love Him more and more and to give yourself to Him, and this fills Him with pride and joy. It is His gaze – full of kindness and encouragement – which you have to learn to receive when you go to adoration.

In order to find out what kind of happiness the Lord wants for you, you must first spend time with Him, talk to Him, listen to Him, "look at Him looking at you," (*Spiritual Exercises of St. Ignatius*, 75) through the face of Christ present in the Blessed Sacrament. What could be better than to contemplate God in the Eucharist as a reminder that God's love for you is love to the point of folly?!

Ideally, try to spend one hour in adoration, because this world is so noisy that it takes time for your heart to find silence and welcome His Presence. One hour may not be possible every day, but aim for several times per week if you want an effective discernment. On other days, try to spend a shorter time (15-20 minutes) in prayer. Regularity is important. What fiancé lets two days go by without calling or meeting up with their beloved?

Testimony of Jessica, age 20:

> Making a commitment to adoration and to faithfulness in prayer has borne tremendous fruit in my discernment process. It has helped me to surrender with trust in my relationship with God, as well as deepen my understanding of the nature of His faithfulness to each of us, enabling me to move forward with confidence.

• GLORIFY God by your life

The quality of prayer also depends on how you live the great command of love in your life. This does not mean you need to measure up to worldly standards of perfection. Such people do not need Jesus, or at least, they don't think they do (Matthew 9:12). Although living a Christian life does not require having mastered the virtues of a canonized saint, it does involve having the desire for holiness. This does not mean living with your head in the clouds (soaring 9,000 feet above the earth, indifferent to everything and everyone), but always keeping your gaze on Heaven as you care for your brothers and sisters on earth. The two standards are very different. By keeping the heaven that awaits you in sight, your eyes are filled with the true Light, and you will know how to distinguish the stars from the street lights!

Looking towards Heaven gives us the insight we need for our life, distinguishing short-term happiness from happiness meant to last. A young woman once asked, "How can you tell the difference between 'Prince Charming' and 'Don Juan just passing through'?" Eternal happiness can be found along the road of Gospel values. You must forego some of the passing pleasures if you believe that these are not your keys to eternity: money, fame, the opinion of others, pleasure, this or that whim. Although these things are not bad in themselves, you know they will never completely fill you with joy, and that you were made for more, for better. Your happiness is beyond these pleasures: it lies in God, who created you, loved you, sanctified you and saved you. He is the one you want to give your life to (even if you are called to marriage or single life). Your life is precious and you do not want to waste it. It is not a video game: you only have ONE LIFE! Which reward is worth the gift of your life? To live the moral life means to live in freedom! This is a condition for good discernment. What prevents people from being truly free is not their weakness, but sin in all its forms. Any sins – lack of love, forgiveness withheld, or addictions – are like enslaving chains around our wrists. You have to be as free as possible in order to follow Jesus. Here are three examples of serious addictions which prevent you from a fruitful discernment:

1. **Alcohol or drugs (marijuana included!)**: Don't risk a "DUI: discerning under the influence." It is too dangerous to go behind the wheel of a car after drinking, so how could someone commit his life if he is "under the influence"? It is obvious that someone who regularly changes his state of consciousness for any reason must get rid of all this before making a major commitment in his life. This applies equally to marijuana, even if it is being legalized in many states.

2. **Sex and pornography**: It is unreasonable to think of getting married or consecrating my celibacy if I am strongly addicted to pornography, sex or masturbation. This is an important point to insist upon, because it is one of the main causes of failure in seeking a vocation. The specialists are only beginning to realize the magnitude of the disaster that Internet pornography is creating today, and the catastrophic consequences for the person.

The physiology of the human brain is such that an image has much more impact than text or even sounds (stronger chemical emission of epinephrine). Through the Internet, the image stimulus is not only passively received (like on TV), but it is also provoked by the user (who clicks on what he wants to see), so that the satisfaction of the desire is not delayed. Unfortunately, this instant gratification provokes very strong addiction or dependence.

The shame, contempt for others (reducing them to an object), aggressiveness, sadness, and solitude involved in this addiction increase the distress, self-hatred, remorse, emptiness and pain, and therefore perpetuate the addiction. The body is not destroyed as it is with tobacco, alcohol, or drugs. The person, however, is quickly and deeply altered in an ability to have relationships that are free, mature, and happy. Hope, joy, and freedom are destroyed.

This is the reason why a young adult who would like to answer a call should be clean from this addiction to porn. A marriage will not last if it is caught in the nets of Internet pornography. Ministry as a priest or as a religious will likewise be quickly stifled and limited.

In a more general way, television, movies and video games can also damage your prayer life, attention span, and inner peace. They can be a means of escaping life and relationships, similar to drugs and alcohol. Many novitiate or diocesan spirituality year programs require a renunciation of TV and Internet for this fundamental time of discernment and growth. Anyone desiring to hear the voice of God more clearly might consider fasting from unnecessary media for a period of time.

To conclude the subject of sexuality and chastity (of body and eyes), let us remember that the same applies to chastity before marriage: it must be clearly understood that two young people having sex before marriage are no longer able to discern the truth of their love, because sexual relationships create a sensual and emotional intimacy that eliminates the distance necessary to be objective. The gift of sexual union affects and distorts all parameters of discernment, like a plane in which all the navigational instruments go crazy, or which is flying too low to find its way. Chastity safeguards purity of the body, but beyond that, it protects the purity of heart and eyes, and therefore the ability to discern. A couple that has not lived chastely ought to take a time of separation and then "start over" and then begin discerning their love after a long time of chastity.

3. Resentment, jealousy, and hatred: These are addictions of the soul. We tend to consider them less serious, but they are just as deadly for our discernment. Here is an example: A young woman cannot discern in peace and truth if she is jealous of her little sister, the "favorite" of the family, who is married to "Mr. Perfect" and already pregnant with her third child. There is also the case of a certain young man: he is in rebellion against his strict and authoritative father (a "soup nazi!") who expects him to have a highly successful career: like father, like son. Is it really in reaction to the father that he chooses total monastic poverty, going around barefoot, with a beard and a buzz? If that is the basis of his call, it is a lie (an act of rebellion, but not a call).

Take another example: Joe should not marry Emily to

get back at Hannah because Hannah dumped him. Nor should Emily become a nun when she realizes that Joe is a jerk. Joe might just start discerning priesthood "as a last resort"! To discern with such motives, listening to wounds, resentment, and jealousy, is a highway leading straight to disaster.

You must begin by striving with the help of God's grace to heal any resentment towards your family, towards this situation or that person, towards God, or maybe even towards yourself before thinking of discerning your call. This reconciliation is vital. It can take a long time, sometimes years, but it is crucial to address any faulty intentions in order to obtain inner peace and integrity of heart before embarking on sound discernment.

In order to discern, you must live an upright life that glorifies God. Of course, no one is perfect, and everyone has many sins to confess. Yet you must be free of deep addictions or hatred that might disturb your spiritual vision, preventing you from hearing the whispers of the Holy Spirit or from seeing the path God wants for your life. These serious sins afflict the heart with "near-sightedness." If you are in this state, you will not see clearly. These sins or addictions act like a computer virus: they take charge of your life, slow you down, prevent you from moving forward, and eventually destroy everything. The best antivirus software for a high-speed connection with God is prayer, Mass, Confession, reading the Bible, adoration... and patience and perseverance.

To put it simply: in order to see clearly, you must try to live according to the Gospel, in true freedom, and to avoid, as much as possible, the kind of nonsense (and sins) that disturb your heart's ability to see.

Luke's testimony (26-year-old), part-time Christian!

For a long time I thought I could live a double life. On Saturday nights, I would go out with my friends; we laughed a lot together, but we also tried out all that life could offer young students in a big city: parties, women, alcohol, not-very-edifying conversations, etc. At the same time, I went to Mass with my family on Sunday mornings (often hung over or half asleep), and I enjoyed going there and praying. I eventually discovered, though, that I was really only a Christian on Sunday, from 11 a.m. to noon! I lived like that for six years, when one day, the Lord and I took a step...

Experience shows that glorifying God with your life will help you move forward, while a double life will only hinder your discernment. These are foundational principles that ground your prayer life and permit God to speak to your heart... in 4G!!! Your conversation with Him – this heart to heart – will become simple and clear. No tunnels will block the reception; no remote forests will put you out of range: your "soul phone" will always have five bars! Your prayer life will be like perfect wifi: secured, fire-walled, high-speed, virus-free, and without interruptions, so that you can download easily, allowing God's voice to manifest itself more clearly in your heart!

It is good to add one last little secret: these four pillars are not easy to live out without the Virgin Mary. The Blessed Mother is a source of help, essential to anyone who wants to recognize, listen and put into practice the call of God in their life. She is a model, a gentle guide. As St. Bernard says, whoever holds Mary's hand has nothing to fear; he will never be lost. So, pull out your rosaries!

2. A sincere desire to give yourself to others

Now that the paths are made straight and the valleys filled, it is important to question the deep motivation behind your call. Before going any further, you have to check – with a sincere heart – that your intention is as pure as possible. It may be evident, but it is still worth mentioning: a core element of discernment is feeling drawn to serve others. Are you already committed to service, good works, or trying to make the lives of others better in some way? What is your commitment to your Church, your friends, or your community? Are you drawn to others? Are you happy to give of yourself, your time and talents for the good of other people?

If you marry Christie, you need to love her, along with the future family you will raise together. It should not be out of self-interest, greed, ambition, to have a trophy wife or for fear of ending up alone. The same with priesthood or religious life: such vocations have to be embraced out of love of neighbor and out of an authentic desire to help people. Without realizing it, you may actually be seeking self-fulfillment, spiritual pride, comfort, or status.

Sometimes a subtle selfishness underlies even our sacrificial sense of duty. We are on a mission to save the world, to solve its problems. When we do something for others, we need to hear that "thank you," feel that pat on the back, see their lives changed. This is noble, but it is not the same as holiness. Pro-active charity that does not seek recognition testifies that it is the Holy Spirit who is at work in your life. As Pope Francis writes, "Works of love directed to one's neighbor are the most perfect external manifestation of the interior grace of the Spirit."[1]

"Directed to your neighbor" means that you do not require or *need* your neighbor's reciprocal love, although, of course, you should hope for it. This might seem obvious, but it is important enough to emphasize here. If your desire to love, help, and serve others comes first, then personal fulfillment and profound happiness will follow; if you are merely seeking your own fulfillment, you will be disappointed.

Testimony of Fr. Tony:

> The first seed of my priestly call came on a mission trip in high school. Our youth group went to help flood victims near St. Louis. The first day, we were introduced to a poor family who had lost everything. We prayed with them, then set to work, gutting their house and shoveling two feet of mud out of their basement. For a week, I totally forgot myself. The filthy, heavy labor was nothing but fun. The last day, exhausted and full of joy, I knew I had to live my life for others.

Here is another quote from Pope Francis: it is "God's love which summons us to mission and makes us fulfilled and productive."[2] Love, altruism, and service are basic ingredients for a healthy and fruitful vocation. The document *Gaudium et Spes* (24), from Vatican II, teaches that "Man, being the only creature created for his own sake, finds himself only in a sincere gift

---

[1] *Evangelii Gaudium*, 37.
[2] *Evangelii Gaudium*, 81.

of himself." We truly find fulfillment through *giving* ourselves to another. If this is the case, you'll be blessed, happy and fruitful wherever you may be.

Is it possible, though, to make a total gift of oneself outside of marriage, priesthood, or religious life? Of course. For some people, their vocation may be to live as a single person in the world (for example as a consecrated virgin or in a secular institute of consecrated life), or even making a private offering of their single state to the Lord. They choose to give themselves to God in this way, consciously trying to create a little monastery around their life and heart where God is glorified, right in the middle of the world.

What about single persons who wanted to get married, but just never found the right soul mate? Or who sought religious life and it never worked out? The universal call to holiness stressed in Vatican II reminds them that their life is anything but meaningless. They are called to the same holiness, the same life of generosity, a full and authentic gift of themselves to others, transforming the world from within in a very challenging way. From this perspective, it is far from a default option!

Often it is single people who can take initiative and make things happen. They tend to have more time, energy, and sometimes money to give themselves in service of God and others. Single people can become examples of great service and generosity. Their single-ness is for them a constant call to generosity, with often more freedom to give of themselves to God and to others on a day-to-day basis.

3. Good friends and mountaintop moments!

"A lonely Christian is a dead Christian!" This quote, although a bit frightening, is a good reminder that it is too difficult to live out your friendship with Jesus alone. Everyone needs to have others around them who bear in their hearts that same desire for holiness. Intense spiritual moments in the company of others like World Youth Day, retreats, pilgrimages, discernment years (ex. School of Life: see Appendix), etc., boost faith and help one avoid walking alone. All of us can be afraid to answer a call from God: Christian living is a daunting task in today's world!

Pope John Paul II understood this well, and in order to encourage young people to be bold, he gathered them together (sometimes even 2 million of them at World Youth Day). "Do not be afraid," he told them. These large gatherings, as well as good friends in Christ, are helpful tools to help you see God's light on your path. They will assist you by giving you courage to move forward. Friends will be more precious than gold for you: "Faithful friends are a life-saving medicine; and those who fear the Lord will find them" (Sirach 6:16). Sirach 6:14 also says that "Faithful friends are a sturdy shelter: whoever finds one has found a treasure." Christian friends are such a treasure because they help us grow in holiness and keep our faith strong!

Katie's testimony (21 years old), an isolated Christian!

> One evening we were at a coffee shop near campus. One of the young men in the group – in front of everyone – announced that he was Christian, that he had given his life to Jesus, and that he did not know

how he could live without Him. Here I had always believed that I was the only young person on campus who wanted to live like that! Brandon – that was his name – introduced me to many other young people like him... like me! There were tons of us!!! Because of them, I found the strength to really live my faith, without shame and without hiding... what a joy! And how much the Lord has helped me grow in my faith since then...

4. Know each state of life: the "Reality Principle"

Once your heart and life is settled in God, then it is time to do some research, guided by the "reality principle." This requires learning a bit about what is special and specific to each state of life. What exactly is life like for a Carmelite nun, a Benedictine monk, a Missionary of Charity or a brother of the Beatitudes? What is the daily schedule for the life of a diocesan priest? What are the blessings and challenges of each vocation in the various dimensions of life: prayer life, studies, the three religious vows (poverty, chastity and obedience), sexual continence, faithfulness in love, apostolate, sacrifice for your brothers/sisters, etc.?

This requires reading and research, and nothing replaces a real encounter. For example, find a way to experience the life by spending some time in a monastery, visiting the communities that interest you, or shadowing a priest for a day. In this discernment, take an objective perspective, lest emotion guide your choice. This requires common sense; you have to be realistic!

The same can be said for marriage. When you fall in love with someone, it is always easy to idealize the romance a bit (or a lot!), seeing the person through rose-tinted glasses. You risk losing touch with the flesh and blood person you believe you love. It is better to keep your feet on the ground. For this, you must get to know their daily life, work, family, friends, passions, and plans. Moreover, in order to be able to love the real "Jeannie" and not just the one you dream of, you need to recognize her weaknesses, too… and know you can live with them. Furthermore, try spending time with a couple whose marriage or family life you admire. Can you picture yourself in their shoes?

Here is Ray's testimony, led by God through all three states of life.

When I was seven, I remember thinking about the deep meaning of life and I can say I received then the deep call to become a religious monk. I wanted to "marry God" and Him alone, not seeing the point about "marrying God's creature" if I could "marry the Creator." I wanted to spend my whole life in this contemplative "heart to heart" with Him alone. I definitely had a contemplative call then. Later on, as a teenager, I saw the point about "marrying God's creature," meaning I saw the point about women (don't ask…)!!! I had a girlfriend for five years, and really felt like starting a Christian family with her, and growing together towards holiness. But the first call was still there, and became more and more pronounced. Therefore, I decided to give two years to God for discernment, going to Ivory Coast, Africa for a Catholic mission. There, the call to celibacy for the Kingdom came back strongly, but I also discovered how much people need the sacraments, and thus decided to become a priest, in order to address this need. I've been a priest for ten years now, and I'm so thankful to God for how He guided me with wisdom and patience, showing me the unique beauty of all these three different calls.

How can you know if you are in the right condition to continue on to Part II and start discerning? Look at the fruits in your heart: If these fruits are peace and joy, they show the faithfulness of the Holy Spirit, and therefore the plan of God for your life. You can move on to Part II.

If, however, you are too bothered by worries, paralyzed with the fear of making a mistake, depressed by your solitude, enslaved by an addiction... take your time, and plunge deeper into God and into prayer. Maybe you have not yet trimmed all of the branches that need cutting. Go at your own pace, but keep on walking. Ask for help, there is nothing to be ashamed of. Find a spiritual director, or a helpful religious community. Talk to a priest or a consecrated sister. Make a spiritual retreat. Never give up or settle for less! If you take a break, God will wait for you, but you must keep on walking!

II

The Discernment Process,
with Three Essential Criteria

How do I know my vocation? Monk, religious, priest, nun, marriage, single life? Many voices are speaking both within me and around me. Here are *three essential criteria* upon which you can rely:

1. Listen to the deepest desire of your heart

You are baptized. That's not just a dusty diploma at the bottom of a sacristy drawer! Baptism means something very concrete: the Holy Spirit dwells in you, and if you pray, you will hear Him whispering in the depths of your heart. He whispers to you of His infinite love, that He has always loved you and always will. He reminds you of who you really are: a son or daughter of the King, infinitely precious to the Father and completely unique.

This means that by listening to God speak in the *depths of your heart,* you will know which happiness He has prepared for you. You have to pay attention to this "deepest desire of your heart," because that is where the Holy Spirit is whispering. He is speaking to your heart in specific ways: it is this desire that tells you where God wants you, because your will is made for His. What is the ideal life you want to live?

Before going any further, it is important to clear up one potentially confusing situation: it is NORMAL to sometimes have contradictory desires within you. As so many young Christians have mentioned, "I have a desire to be consecrated to God, but at the same time, I want to start a family and have children."

25

To sort through this, ask yourself some questions. Which of these desires is deeper? What would your dream life be for the next 30 years, if you had to write it out today? Are there a wife (or husband) and children in the picture? Are you surrounded by like-minded people in community? An exciting apostolate which brings the love of God to hundreds who wouldn't otherwise receive it? A hidden life of prayer and contemplation?

Any future priest, in fact, should have thought about and even desired marriage. It is not a good sign if this has never even occurred to him. It is healthy if he wanted to start a family, but discovered at a deeper level that he wanted to serve God without the mediation of a wife and children as in the life of a priest. Similarly, it does not bode well for the nun who chose this path because she could not stand the idea of a man!!

It is normal and healthy to feel drawn in different directions at the same time. But in the depths of your heart and in your conscience, God will speak to you; it is the deepest desire that you should follow, the one that fills you with the most joy and peace.

So you have to "listen to your heart." This is the most important criterion. Now you can understand why the conditions of the first chapter were so important to fulfill: a regular prayer life, the sacraments, the Bible, freedom from sin, etc. To return to the Internet analogy, if your connection is not high-speed and secure, it is better not to download anything at all. If you do not know who sent you an e-mail, do not open the attachment! Without a thorough job of preparing your heart and your life, that is, without meeting the conditions set out in Part I, it is prudent to doubt the deepest desire of your heart.

You might be blinded by fears, resentment, pride, ego, or many other frivolous or short-lived reasons.

A similar method of discernment

During Ignatian retreats, the following spiritual exercise is sometimes suggested for those who hesitate between marriage and priesthood (or consecrated life). Imagine that you have chosen marriage. Think of yourself married, a husband, a father of a family, your wife, your children, your witness in the workplace, your prayer life, your pastimes... and how your life will be in five years, ten, forty, when the kids reach the teenage years, when they are off to college and the nest is empty, when you are retired and outlive your spouse... Imagine the details of your life, its joys, trials, challenges, rewards...

You can even write out the scenario. Keep this thought in mind for three to five days, putting the other vocational possibility completely out of your head. What do you feel? Peace and joy, or rather anxiety and stress?

Next, do the same exercise focused on the other hypothesis: take several days and imagine yourself as a priest or religious. What is your ministry like, your parish, your community, your daily celebration of the Mass, your mission of charity and witness, your prayer, your life of self-offering and intimacy with Jesus, your private prayer, praying the Divine Office, and hobbies living alone? Or as a religious, your common meals and prayer, chanting the Office, missions or formation abroad, friendships, recreation, and struggles with your brothers and sisters? Then retired in your nursing home or community, receiving your spiritual children for spiritual direction. Now what are the fruits in your heart?

It is a helpful discernment tool to see yourself so concretely in each call, one after the other, and to imagine yourself in the years to come. Next, write your own "hagiography," your own story of holiness, as we find written about the saints of bygone centuries. Leaving aside your fears and the pressure you feel from family and friends, what is the life of your dreams?

What we are looking for is a vision of life that brings the most interior peace. Your call will give you peace. St. Gregory of Nazianzus used to say to the Lord: "Your will is my peace." Let it be your motto.

2. Test the "endurance" of this deepest desire

A second criterion, which goes hand in hand with the first, is the "endurance" of the call. How long has this desire been the deepest one in your heart? Eight days? Six months? Two years? A true call withstands the test of time, and does not waver with the changing seasons, or with the attractiveness of the new guy or gal next door! Sometimes the call takes root in childhood.

Many boys experience the desire to be a priest and to "play Mass." This desire call is often motivated by reasons that are a bit infantile, like the beautiful chasuble the priest wears. This is normal, considering the innocent heart of a child; nevertheless, it could be a call, and the Lord can use this to awaken in the child a spiritual curiosity. Later on, the Lord will speak with firmness and depth to the maturing heart.

We might say the same for marriage. How many little girls "play mom," and cart their dolls around to practice caring for them? The persistence of this desire is what counts.

God speaks with faithfulness, and this also means that neither thorns, nor hardened soil, nor famished birds will prevent that seed of a call from growing deep down. It is like a diamond hidden in a field: the field can be flooded or desolate, but the diamond will still remain inside, waiting to be discovered. It is as if, in a certain way, our call does not belong to us, that it comes from further away and from deeper down than we ourselves can fathom, and yet we have longed for it always.

Typically, it seems that if childhood has awakened the first intuition of a religious call, this sense will return again around age 20 or 25. At this season in life, you find yourself with "your life in your own hands" (Psalm 119). You need to use this freedom to move towards a lifelong commitment. There is a temptation to just "take advantage" of this freedom, instead of taking the steps towards a mature choice of life. As it turns out, if you cannot come up with a way to use your freedom, life will choose for you. Many religious orders have age limits and prefer candidates between 20-30 years old. Little by little, the dating pool gets smaller as others marry. If you cannot summon up the courage to declare your love for Juliet, the Romeo down the street will come and sweep her off her feet. If you perpetually hesitate between religious life and marriage, life will choose for you: you'll remain single, but not by choice!

Time confirms a call, but wise delay should not turn into a paralyzing procrastination at the hands of your fears. Often we meet couples who are "eternal fiancés," who have been together for years and just cannot tie the knot. Generally speaking, this is not a good sign. If Juliet were truly the gal of your dreams, you would have just one preoccupation: to marry her! All the rest would be but details – salary, home, etc.

Here is one way to unravel such situations: if you have already been dating or engaged for several years, and you or your fiancé still cannot make a decision, take a break for three months, cold turkey. Abstain from all contact: from seeing each other, calls, texts, e-mails, facebook, tweets, even handwritten letters… and set up a date for three months down the road. This distance, solitude and, of course, prayer, will help you see your relationship more clearly. If it is really Mister or Miss Right, then at the end of three months apart, it should be obvious. If, however, you were peaceful without them in your life, perhaps this person is not "the one."

Testimony of Karen, wife of Matt:

> Matt and I had been dating for nine years. I loved him too much to break it off, but all the while I was aware of getting older and knew I wanted to have children! There were always excuses why we weren't married yet and time was slipping away. In the end, someone advised us to try a dating fast. We went cold turkey for four months, and in the end, he proposed! We are now happily married with three children.

When a dating relationship gets too long, too intimate, or too physical, another healthy step to take, *before* getting engaged, is the first step of Catholic marriage preparation. This first step, before Marriage and NFP classes, involves a conversation about the compatibility and communication of the couple. In most dioceses and parishes, this is based around the FOCUS exam. The format feels a bit like the SAT, but the content of the test involves all different dimensions of a nuptial relationship: communication, family values, perceptions of one another, relationships with potential in-laws and friends, raising children, anxieties and annoyances, understanding of the marriage covenant, finances, faith, affection and sexuality, religious practice, spirituality, daily habits, wounds of the past, etc.

The results of the test become a conversation starter for a series of meetings with a priest or lay minister. These conversations reveal so many things on which to base your discernment. Usually, however, engaged couples are preoccupied with jobs, studies, and wedding plans. Moreover, they have already announced a "save the date" to all their family and friends. The discernment seems over. Unfortunately, there is often further discerning to be done, but there is too much pressure of each other's expectations as well as wedding plans already in process. This all inhibits the climate of freedom necessary to continue asking deep questions and sharing honest thoughts. It is precisely that freedom, however, that is required of a valid (and a happy) marriage.

Take these careful steps, but keep in mind that discernment never gives us 100% clarity. Vows do not come with money-back guarantees. But if you have prepared well, you can make your vows, marital or religious, with great confidence. From that moment on, you need to be able to say, through thick and thin, "I walked the road of discernment with sincerity and integrity. Despite all my limits and sins, I took the steps necessary for a good discernment. If you, Lord, have permitted me to come to this moment (vows, ordination, marriage…), I can be confident that this is the path that you marked out for me. The time of doubting is over."

3. The "Reality Principle" revisited: it is the Church who calls; it is Brian who proposes

There is a third criterion for discernment, and this one is not up to you, but rather depends on the "external reality." Here comes the famous "reality principle" once again. If you are called to marry Tú-Trinh, it is not enough to have known it since first grade, and to desire her more than all the others. She has to agree with it, too! And God needs to confirm in her heart the same love that you feel. If she has no feelings for you, sorry bud – she's not the love of your life and bride-to-be.

A priest tells the story of when he was having lunch with Christian music pioneer Michael W. Smith. After pulling out a photo of his wife, Michael explained how they met: "I was just sitting in the office, and suddenly a beautiful woman walked through and went into the rest-room. Immediately I picked up the phone, called my mom, and told her I had just seen the girl I was going to marry. What's her name? She asked. I don't know, I said, but I'll go and find out!" Sure enough, Michael and Debbie got married in 1981 and are still together today!

This proves love at first sight is a possibility. This dream-come-true, however, was more than just imaginary love. If Debbie had not been interested in Michael too, the situation could have quickly been creepy. The rest of their story probably had to do with getting to know each other, examining their hearts respectively, and moments of openness to the Holy Spirit. The lightning bolt of love can draw you towards someone, but unless it is grounded in reality and mutual love, it might be just a fairy tale.

If you are called to be a priest, the same applies. It is the Church who calls and who sends the workers into the vineyard. This is why your call needs to be discerned equally, and even firstly, by the Church, that is to say, by a priest, a spiritual director, a vocations director, a seminary, or a bishop! The Church is a good mother, and her generous heart knows that the Lord provides for what He commands, that He completes the work He begins in the hearts of His children. Peter was far from perfect, but the Lord, in an instant, called him and chose him to build the foundation for His Church.

It can seem like failure if you pursue a young woman, a religious order, or the priesthood, and are "turned down." It may also be the Lord's way of showing you a different path, as when the Spirit turned Paul back from his attempt at a mission (Acts 16:6). Such a case was recounted in a lunch table encounter with Tom Monahan, at the time the CEO of Domino's Pizza.

At fifteen young Tom felt a priestly call and entered a high-school seminary. He was kicked out and never even graduated. He and his brother still wanted to do something for the Lord, so they took over a failing pizza joint and called it Domino's (which in Latin means "for the Lord"). The Domino's logo, he explained, has a two and a one, symbolizing Jesus' one person and two natures. At the same time, it is two plus one to symbolize the Trinity. The Lord used that generous heart, docile to the word of his rector, not only to bring pizza to doorsteps around the globe, but also to bring about the number one Catholic benefactor in America.

Have the courage to ask a priest to sit down and talk with you about your call. If you are a young woman and you are feeling an attraction or some recurring thoughts towards religious life, find a nun to talk to. If you are discerning marriage, talk to a married couple you admire, and visit their house. Also keep in mind that priests and religious hold a lot of insight about the lay vocation. They are called to be "specialists in the knowledge of the human heart." Although they may have never been married, they have listened to dozens, maybe hundreds of lay people open their hearts and share their desires and fears, hopes and wounds.

A meeting for spiritual counsel, or an ongoing relationship of spiritual direction, is not aimed at letting someone else show you the way or make your decision. The spiritual director is there not so much to direct you as to accompany you, to help you speak your heart in the presence of the Holy Spirit, to help you hear yourself more objectively, to be a reference point and encouragement as you take one step at a time. Choose your director well. Find one with whom you feel truly free. Choose wisely the way you share your heart with a director, with family, and with close friends. Watch out for leaking onto Facebook what you should be penning in your diary and waiting to share in that precious moment of spiritual direction. "Let those who are friendly to you be many, but one in a thousand your confidant" (Sirach 6:6).

III

Discernment Firewall:
Five Pitfalls to Avoid

Since they lack natural strength,
they think themselves full of grace.
Since they lack the courage of this world,
they think they are of God.

Charles Peguy, referring to certain priests

Since they do not love people,
they think they love God.

St. Teresa of Avila, referring to certain nuns

These two quotes seem harsh but are quite accurate in some cases. The point of these spiritual authors is that you cannot choose a vocation by default, as if it were Plan B. You cannot be a nun simply out of disinterest for men, or a priest for fear of married life. You cannot marry Juan because José will never fall for you or because now he is taken... or simply for fear that otherwise, you might never get married.

So here is a rule of discernment: never be ruled by your fears! Do not ignore them, which could be reckless, but face them and seek to understand them. It may be a question of getting in touch with your own weakness or it may be a legitimate fear of a path that is too dangerous. Often, we think that the most difficult way is what will bring God the most glory. If you are afraid, however, of the call to be a missionary in the Amazon or to be an undercover preacher in China, this might be a sign that it is not your call.

Fears, however, seldom come from God, and often are products of wounds from the past. They frequently come from Satan, or at least he amplifies them. Satan wants your unhappiness. He would like to see life pass you by, to see you give up on your holiness. His main weapon is fear. Will you let your life be ruled by your fears, or rather by faith and trust in God?

This chapter will unmask five common pitfalls in which your choices can be hijacked by fear, illusion, or anxiety:

1. By hiding yourself in a dream in order to avoid making a choice

2. By hiding yourself in the busyness of short-term goals in order to avoid the deeper decisions

3. By hiding yourself in a failure in order to avoid the battle

4. By hiding yourself behind God in order to avoid taking responsibility

5. By hiding behind what others want for you

1. The "Inception" Syndrome: living in your dream world

"Say the words 'my life,' then try and hold back your tears." The French poet, Louis Aragon, coined these frightening words. Indeed, how many people fail to live the life they desire? They heard the call, but it got tangled in the thorns of life... shyness, fear, laziness, pleasures, addictions, bad advice, or even worse, one's dreams. How many people dream their life and never live out their dreams?

We all know that there is a crisis of commitment today. In our global world, everything is possible, and choosing is ever more difficult. We are fed so many models of happiness and success that we are paralyzed by the fear of ruining our life or "missing the boat." If my life does not resemble a fairy tale film, I must be doing something wrong. But that is fiction, and our lives are non-fiction!

Films often give us a false portrait of true love. Because of all these virtual models of the perfect life, young people can have a standard of happiness and success that is illusory. Not reaching the expectations they have set for their lives, more and more young people flee to virtual worlds (video games, social networks, movies...) or even worse to modified states of consciousness (alcohol, drugs, marijuana, etc.).

Many times, movies reveal a generation's mindset and morals. How many blockbusters have involved plots about an alternative reality or a dream: *The Matrix, Surrogates, Avatar, Inception, Tron, Avalon*... The hero is "more or less" there – as an avatar or a surrogate – but their body, even their consciousness, is elsewhere, and even the dream is perhaps but a dream within a dream within a dream, within a dream... We could also include here all the fantasy movies, the role-play video games, etc., but that would take us too long.

Dreams, virtual worlds, alternative realities – all of these are ways to avoid commitment, choosing instead to live an *"e-life"*! It means wishing life were like a video game that has the safety of the reset button, or a computer that, if it crashes, can just be rebooted. Dreaming can be a symptom of our fear of commitment, fear of real life.

Many analysts explain that emotional fear of relationship and commitment is somehow linked to the success of Facebook in our culture: people project themselves via webcam into relationships which become their very own movie. You can just show part of yourself, filter out whatever you want, "like" whoever asks you to "like" them. You create your "dream self" and only the relationships you "like," and you can simply unsubscribe when you get tired of it all. When God the Father saved us, however, He didn't send His avatar on earth to do so, but His only begotten Son.

In the reality and real relationships of a Christian vocation, your alter ego dissipates and you are left with yourself, with particular sins and acts of charity that are concrete. It's about you, the true you, not your "profile," not your "tweet," not your "avatar" or "login." Underneath the *e*-identity and the artificial make-up, beyond the dream, it's you, with your real wounds, but also your real, lasting virtues, hopes, joys and friendships.

Nobody wants to suffer, and of course the heart is the most sensitive of all. To love is to open your heart to another human being or to God, and exposing yourself is always difficult, sometimes even terrifying. You might be hurt sometimes, you might be misled or betrayed, you might be humiliated, but at the end of your life, you'll be able to say: I loved. I really loved. That was me, loving so and so. The true me, not an avatar or a profile, and therefore I have no regrets. I lived my life to the full.

A new generation of young people is fond of online relationships and evermore distracted from real, face-to-face contact. Beeps and rings can be heard in almost any public place. Two hours per day: this is the average time Americans spend on their cell phones.[3] Two hours: that's one full month 24/7 at the end of the year!

A certain group of friends tried to fight back by playing a game when they go out to lunch: see who can resist the longest from the distraction of their iPhone. They put their phones in the center of the table as they order and begin to eat. The first to answer a call or check a text picks up the lunch tab!

But is there really anything new under the sun? Jesus' contemporaries were also numbed to His call to authentic love:

---

[3] Survey of the C.E.A. (Consumer Electronic Association), Sept. 18, 2013.

"To what shall I compare this generation? They are like children seated in the marketplace, singing, 'We played the flute for you, and you did not dance; we sang a dirge, and you did not weep...'" (Matthew 11:16). In each of us, there is that neglected child, buried in the cocoon of his headphones, who dares not take a step out of himself, to dance or play or even shed a tear. To live your life means risking what might happen if you live it to the full. Among all those media lovers glued to their screens, pods and pads, there are certainly little St. Dominics and little Mother Teresas somewhere. And God needs saints *today*.

You want that happiness *today*. But you need to say "yes" to His call; you need to break the bubble of your online profile and cross the threshold of real life. And how will you hear that call if you never take off your headphones?

Here's a little text of the theologian Hans Urs von Balthasar that sums it up:

> The eye that looks at me fixedly always says, "Today: it is now that I want to be loved." But I lower my eyes and say: "I will love you tomorrow."
>
> "I'm coming, I'm coming right away!", the child cries out to his mother when she calls him in, and he finishes playing his game, thinking that surely obedience includes a certain period of grace – a human margin. Who could all at once make a clean break with his life?
>
> And if I must nevertheless feel the pain of separation, then at least yield on this point and make me this concession: you may take me tomorrow if you'll only let me have today. I am even prepared to take

up your cross, to follow your Way of the Cross, station after station to the end, to the complete sacrifice and the definitive death – under one condition, that is: let it be tomorrow.[4]

To this, God responds (in this beautiful text of an unknown author), asking us not to wait any longer to start loving Him and living our life to the full:

Love Me just as you are.

I know your misery, the struggles, the afflictions of your soul, the weakness of your body.

I am also aware of your cowardice and your sins, but nevertheless I tell you: Give Me your heart, love Me just as you are!

If you wait to become an angel before you devote yourself to love, you will never love Me.

Although you are faint-hearted in fulfilling your obligations and in practicing a virtuous life, although you often fall back into the sins which you would not like to commit any more, I will not allow you not to love Me. Just love Me as you are!

In every moment and in whatever situation you find yourself, in eagerness and dryness, when you are faithful or unfaithful to me, love Me just as you are!

I desire the love of your poor heart, for if you wait until you are perfect, you will never love Me.

Could I not make a precious seraph out of a little grain of sand, radiating purity, noble-mindedness and love?

---

[4]   H.U. von BALTHASAR, *Heart of the World*, Ignatius Press, 1954, pp. 96-98.

Am I not the Almighty? And when it pleases Me to leave those wonderful beings in Heaven and to prefer the love of your poor heart – am I not always the Lord of My Love?

My child, allow Me to love you. I want your heart.

I will certainly change you in the course of time, but today I love you just as you are, and I wish that you also love Me just as you are.

I want to see the rising of your love out of your deepest misery. I also love the weakness in you.

I love the love of the poor and the humble ones.

I want that unceasing call coming out of your miseries: "Jesus, I love You!"

I request only this song of your heart. I do not need your wisdom, nor your talents.

One thing alone is important to Me: To see you working with love! It is not your virtues I am desiring, for if I had given you such, you were so weak as to nourish your selfish love with them.

But do not bother about this. I could have made you something greater, but you will be the useless servant. I will even take away the little you possess, because I created you for love.

Today, I am standing at the gate of your heart like a beggar – I, the King of Kings! I knock and wait – hurry up to open for Me! Do not plead your misery, for if you would know fully your spiritual poverty, you would die from pains. What would wound My heart would be to see you doubt Me and lose confidence in Me. I also desire that the smallest dealing

you undertake, you do it out of love. I count on you
to please Me.

Do not bother that you do not possess virtues. I will
give you Mine. When you have to suffer, I will give
you the strength to stand it. If you offer Me your
love, I will give you so much of it that you understand what it means to love – far more than you can
dream of.

However, remember to love Me just as you are! I
have given you My Mother. Let everything, just everything, go through her pure heart.

Come what may, do not wait to become a saint before you devote yourself to love; for then you would
never love Me.

Another way of hiding from a choice is to want to "have
your cake and eat it too": you walk with a religious community,
while at the same time, you date, because "you never know...?!"
But every choice, every commitment is also a renunciation. To
be an adult means to renounce all of one's childhood dreams, in
order to choose from among them the brightest prospect.

It was already mentioned that it is normal and healthy to
have all the calls at the same time. You enter seminary, but you
still desire marriage. All the better! It is a good sign, a sign that
you are "healthy." It is a sign that you have a heart that beats,
a body, emotions, sexuality, and so forth. If you were lacking
any desire to marry and have children, it is this that would be a
concern. The desire for marriage should remain all your life, in
a way, even if you become a priest or a nun. On a deeper level,
however, you have the desire to serve God as a priest, or to

consecrate your life completely to God. For this, you renounce marriage and family life. You chose, indeed, to live your dream, or rather to follow the call that is deeper in you.

You can also "dream your life" by choosing a religious order in the way one might choose, for example, a college: making up your mind according to social or human criteria instead of leaving the final call to God alone. Applying to the school with the highest-ranked degree program and planning a career with the best prospects all make sense. However, seeking out the religious order with the most impressive formation program, highest number of vocations, or most successful ministry is not necessarily going to lead you to God's call. There is nothing wrong with using your brain to assess a good fit; yet one responds to God's call with an act of trust in the One who calls.

Choosing a husband or wife, likewise, is an act of faith in God. If this total availability to God is not there in the heart of the one who responds, the gift will not be total. You make a vow "for better or for worse," even if life does not take the path you were expecting. If your spouse has an accident and is paralyzed, he or she remains your spouse.

2. The "Maybe Generation" Syndrome: hiding behind short term goals to avoid deeper decisions

Indecision may or may not be my problem.

(Jimmy Buffett)

Why say "yes" when you can say "maybe"? Why decide now when you can wait a bit longer and see what other opportunities present themselves? Commitment, if we take it seriously, can be downright intimidating – especially when it involves a lifelong commitment or vow. Pursuing short-term goals in order to sidestep the real issues is a way to hide behind a "maybe."

"Let your 'Yes' mean 'Yes,' and your 'No' mean 'No'" (Matthew 5:37). The problem is that saying yes now implies saying no to everything else that may come along, and we don't want to miss out! Just think for a minute about Facebook and other e-vites. Once upon a time, when people were invited to a party, they had to RSVP either yes or no to let the host adequately prepare. Now, there are three viable options: "yes" and "no," (both of which imply a firm decision), and the ever-so-tempting "maybe" option, which often represents half of the guests' answers.

Saying "maybe" means different things to different people. For some, it is a stall tactic – to see if a better offer comes around. For others, it is a softer way of saying no, or it gives a last minute way out if needed. "A 'maybe' protects us from being a promise-breaker," says Gerald Goodman, professor emeritus of clinical psychology at UCLA. The problem is that it also prevents us from committing to relationships. If your mother had answered "maybe" to your father's proposal, you wouldn't be reading this book today!

This widespread "maybe" response has led to today's young adults being nicknamed the "Maybe Generation." What does "maybe" actually mean...? In the case of an e-vite, "maybe" means "I will go... if nothing better comes along, depending on who else is going, if I am not too tired, if I am in the mood, or even if I finish painting my room in time, etc." In other words, it means I do not have to make a decision... yet. Never mind that the host has no idea how many hot dogs and hamburgers to grill. Never mind if the birthday girl has no idea if she should reserve a table for twelve at the restaurant or for four... if I do not HAVE to make a commitment, why shouldn't I keep my freedom until the very last minute? Yet our freedom is meant to allow us to choose the happiness God wants to give us, and this involves a commitment of love. It is an illusion that freedom from commitment will lead us to real love or real happiness.

Short-term goals, it is true, can help us avoid staying idle or rushing into a lifelong commitment too hastily. They can be stepping stones to launch us into our vocation. The pitfall lies in letting short-term goals take up our time, until suddenly five years have passed and I am no closer to my vocation! Every year there are students who, nearing graduation without really knowing which career to pursue, decide to get another degree instead to buy more time. This does not eliminate the decision; it just puts it off. A choice still needs to be made.

For young people discerning a religious vocation, seeking short-term commitments in ministry can be a mask for indecision. Mission trips, service years, formation programs, theology degrees... all are positive activities for young Catholics, unless they just become a way of hiding from the deeper decision. Giving a year to the Lord is beautiful, but it is no substitute for giving a lifetime.

Ministry can be a good way to become more familiar with the Church and with different spiritualities. It can help you get to know priests and religious. Hanging around them can make you feel holy, inspire you, or help you radically practice your faith, but you might ask yourself the question of whether you are trying to live vicariously through them rather than decide and commit to your own path of holiness. You might find yourself with a growing devotion to Our Lady of Perpetual Discernment. Meanwhile, the seasons pass. Even though five years of mission work are praiseworthy, if it is not a step towards your deeper vocation, then it too can become a way of hiding. Ask yourself: am I making real steps toward my vocation? Are my current activities and relationships building something that corresponds to my deeper call? What do I plan to do after my short-term projects are over?

The same works for marriage. If you discover that the person you are dating is not who you want to marry, it is better to break it off and move on. Do not waste years in a dead-end relationship, hoping that "maybe" he will change, or fearing that "maybe" nothing better will come along. This is fear and it will keep you from your true love! Rebecca and Joe, after dating seriously for four years, may find a litany of short-term reasons not to get engaged (money, getting settled in careers, too busy, etc.). Sometimes these reasons are valid; other times it is just fear surfacing and putting off the real decision. This is not to say that we should jump in and make rash decisions, or commit before we have come to a mature decision. The problem is that time is slowly ticking, and if Joe and Rebecca do NOT belong together, it is important to move on to find the right person.

3. The "Finding Nemo" Syndrome: letting the failures keep you down

Where else can you hide from yourself? In your failures. The problem here is spiritual impatience. You want it your way, right away. "Dear God, grant me patience and I want it right now!" says the joke, but we often pray that way. Click here for the high-speed download. But reality doesn't sync in just one click, and often, you really need to battle through obstacles.

To take a biblical example, read the book of the prophet Jonah again, noticing how he wants to give up on God's will and instructions, getting discouraged at each obstacle. He ends up under the sea in the abyss of his own self-pity. The frustration of Jonah can also be found down below, in the animated movie *Finding Nemo*. With new obstacles arising every five minutes, the two main characters are always tempted to give up. In the end, however, they find what they are looking for: their beloved Nemo.

This spiritual strength is what Jesus calls perseverance, and it saves our lives, He says repeatedly: "By your perseverance you will gain your lives" (Luke 21:19). It is the opposite of being that straw blown away by the wind (Job 21:18). Every call will have its moments of discouragement, battle, and exhaustion. Just when we think we have arrived at the goal, at a point of grace and satisfaction, the battle continues. St. Augustine said, "Once you have found Him, seek Him still, for He is immense" (*Treatise on John*, 63:1).

Discouragement is the worst of all evils in the spiritual life. Tell yourself that each day is an entirely new day, starting from square one. If you make a decision to never get discouraged, victory will be certain. Doing so, the clock will be in your favor. Learn to live the present moment, and in due time you will find your call and you will live it out. Your perseverance and determination, however, must be 100%.

This means that you must choose to NEVER be ruled by your fears. It is normal to have these fears sometimes, but you cannot let your fears run your life. The following are four types of fear that young people often face on the path to God:

• *Fear of God*

We are often afraid of God, that is, of what He might ask of us. We think to ourselves that if we give our life to the Lord, it will necessarily involve a life of sacrifice and suffering, a painstaking way of the cross. This discourages so many people. Even if some have the courage to step up to the challenge, if they have this mindset, they are still mistaken. So goes the story of the young woman, who made vows because she believed that "the choice of God must be the most difficult choice." This was the skewed interpretation of the parable of the narrow door (and years later, the woman left the convent).

How many young women think that they must sacrifice their happiness for God's sake? God does not want to crucify us; He wants to rescue us and give us life! The true call fills you with joy and enthusiasm; it sets you at ease, in peace, allowing you to be yourself. You should not have to force your personality to fit into your call. The call should feel natural, although with the awareness of the need for grace and for growth over time. You should have a sense of confidence, knowing that God transforms and equips us when we follow Him. The call is, in fact, the most easy and natural way for you to make it to heaven. The vocation someone is not called to is what should end up seeming difficult and threatening. It is possible, for example, that a priest might be amazed by a father of a big family and feel incapable of such a task. When God calls, He is asking for nothing more of you than yourself. Rather, it is He who gives, and gives again, and fills us with love. Afterward, when life's inevitable trials come along, it is better to have God at the heart of your life, for He will strengthen you in the midst of trials.

• *Fear of Oneself*

Another common fear is the fear of yourself, fear of your own weaknesses. How many young men hesitate to enter seminary because they are shy, they have not learned to speak well in public, or they are not good students? How many young women discern consecrated life in order to hide from men, from their femininity, even from marriage itself? How many others are simply afraid of their own sexuality and emotions?

Fears and weaknesses are part of our humanity. However, these fears and personal weaknesses should not keep us from a profound and authentic call. We should surpass these obstacles. It is possible! It takes prayer, patience (that means time, too!), and the help of friends, spiritual directors, sometimes even counselors. We need help to distinguish what is personal weakness from what is an "impediment." Personal weaknesses – shyness, slow learning, sexual and emotional fragility, etc. – should not be obstacles for the call of God. On the contrary, often

God uses our weaknesses to bear fruit in our lives and mission. "When I am weak, then I am strong," says St. Paul (2 Corinthians 12:10), who understood that it is precisely in the midst of poverty when we are unable to count on ourselves, on our own strengths and talents, that we learn to abandon ourselves to the Lord and allow His Spirit to work through us.

There are many new priests who are so petrified to speak in public that they spend hours preparing homilies; over time, they can become some of the best preachers!

An "impediment" is something different. These are rarer, and if you have one, you must do your best to accept it with faith and peace and let your life take a different direction, confident that your path to holiness lies elsewhere, and that the Lord did not abandon you. These impediments go back to the "principle of reality" explained earlier. Here are some examples: the Church teaches that a young man cannot be a priest if he has "deep seated homosexual tendencies."[5] It is considered as an impediment to priesthood. How to understand "deep seated" is a delicate matter, and thus this situation needs to be discussed on a one-to-one basis with a vocation advisor. Keep in mind that such an impediment has nothing to do with whether or not someone will become a saint! As for marriage, the most common impediment will be young age, consanguinity, or the lack of physical capacity for consummation.

---

[5] *"Instruction concerning the Criteria for the Discernment of Vocations with regard to Persons with Homosexual Tendencies in view of their Admission to the Seminary and to Holy Orders,"* Vatican Congregation for Catholic Education (11/4/2005).

• *Fear of Wounds*

There is also the fear of wounds you might have suffered in the past. Many fears, in fact, are a result of painful past experiences. For example, there is the young woman who was head-over-heels for a guy and opened her heart to him. He, in turn, took advantage of her, used her, and abused her. She was left so deeply wounded that she resolved never again to open her heart to a guy, and so she entered the convent. Instead of listening for a call, she listened to her wound. Another common case is the young man with a real call to the priesthood, who after a painful or unpleasant experience with a priest, simply calls it quits with discernment.

• *Fear of Getting it Wrong*

This fear was already mentioned in the last chapter, and it will be addressed again at the end of the book.

4. The "Superman" Syndrome: waiting for a sign from God

When worries creep in about getting it wrong, it can be tempting to ask God for signs to reveal your destiny. This may be veiled in pious words of faith, obedience, and abandonment to God's will. In reality, though, you may be waiting indefinitely for the requested sign to appear, piercing the skies to save you like Superman. However, this can be a subtle way of shirking responsibility, and, meanwhile, losing freedom, the essential element of any commitment.

One way we can gamble with God is by jumping to conclusions when coincidences occur. For example, there was a man who loved cars. When he converted, the Lord called him to give them up and drive a more practical car. A few years went by, and one day he kept seeing and admiring a Lexus. He was on his way to get a haircut, and he prayed, "Lord, I think you are leading me back to my love for cars, and so unless you give me a clear sign otherwise, I'll take it as your will that I should buy a Lexus." At the barber shop, he sat down to wait, and picked up the first magazine on the coffee table. It had a nice red Lexus, but with a title that read "The Diabolic Lexus."

God does not always make things so clear! We can cast lots, saying, "If John wears his orange sweater tomorrow, Lord, I'll know he is Mr. Right"; or "The first nun I see will be the community for me." God simply does not work like that, apart from some very, very rare exceptions.

Sign-searching can mean we are "putting God to the test," and God does not usually intervene Superman-style. He does not often arrive with bells and whistles to aid our distress. Sure God speaks to us (through prayer, *lectio*, pilgrimages, encounters, or the events of life), but He rarely turns our lives upside-down overnight, and rarely grants visions that map out our entire story. That is not to say it never happens; there is more than one St. Paul who's been knocked off his horse in the history of salvation. However, God intervenes this way when the soul is prepared in one way or another, and thus ready for it.

For example, the Lord already knew St. Paul's zeal for seeking the truth, even though it was misguided. Other saints have similar stories, but the principle is the same: God never violates our freedom or forces His will on us. He never makes the decision for us. What kind of father would do so? Moreover, when He gets us out of a pickle or enlightens the way, He often makes sure we have our share of the struggle first. How else would we grow?

Another way we look for signs is playing Bible roulette. We open the Bible at random to find *the* answer from God in the first verse we put our finger on. Not only is this a denial of our freedom, but it also sounds a lot like putting God to the test. Yes, turn to His Word, but do not expect God to break out a magic wand. He offers us His Word, He guides us or confirms the direction we've taken, but He never uses it as a substitute for our liberty.

A much safer practice is consistent *lectio divina*, through which God educates our freedom and speaks to our hearts in little and big ways each day. "God's Word is unpredictable in its power" says Pope Francis, who also reminds us that the Word of God grows in our lives like a seed, over time, even as the farmer sleeps (Mark 4:26-29).[6] God will guide you each time you open the Bible, but only occasionally does He give gift-wrapped solutions on demand. The fundamental principle is that He never chooses in your place.

Also, your intelligence and will have to be fully utilized in your discernment process. God responds and blesses our efforts when we use these faculties to seek His will. Your freedom is His gift, and God does not take back His gifts. He expects you to use them, according to your conscience, and for the good.

---

[6] *Evangelii Gaudium*, 22.

Here lies your dignity. To hide behind a sign is like abdicating your freedom, abandoning your life merely to chance. It can be a sign of spiritual laziness, an escape, and in the end a dangerous delusion. God may send signs to call you, to lead you on, to confirm your decisions. God might help you to meet the right people, to hear a Scripture verse, to get a job interview, to find the right place for retreat or prayer. But He will never make the choice for you. Nothing, in fact, can force your freedom, which is His gift to you. What father would choose in the place of his own children? God loves us and desires that we step out in freedom, step into mature adulthood. Herein lies our dignity.

5. The "Titanic" Syndrome: bad advice from good friends

In 2012, an Australian nurse named Bonnie Ware wrote a book about her experience with her dying patients. This book, *The Top Five Regrets of the Dying*, quickly became a best-seller. Do you know what the first regret is? "I wish I'd had the courage to live a life true to myself, not the life others expected of me." How interesting and sad at the same time! This was the most common regret of all. It indicates that many people do not live a life true to themselves, but rather are ruled by peer-pressure, social conventions, or simply what their family expected from them. What a shame. When people realize that their life is almost over and look back, it is easy to see how many dreams have gone unfulfilled. Most people have not honored even half of their dreams. They have just let themselves be carried away by life's current, succumbing to social, financial, or family pressure. To follow a call, you not only need courage, but also good advisers and, above all, true freedom in your relationships with your friends and family. Not only do you need a spiritual director who knows what he is doing, but you must also be on guard for the right counsels that your friends and family members may offer. You need to receive their words of wisdom with a certain detachment and objectivity. In *Downton Abbey*, as in many romantic tales, from *Jane Eyre* to *Titanic* to *West Side Story*, true love clashes with social barriers. Lady Sybil (Jessica Brown Findlay) withstands all the pressure of her English aristocratic family to discourage her love with Branson, the family's chauffeur (and an Irishman on top of that!), whom she loves despite the scandal caused by their difference on the social ladder. Time reveals that their love is real, and although they face many trials, their courage and perseverance bring them together in a happy marriage.

Despite their wisdom and good will, family and friends are sometimes obstacles to our deep desires and call. It is all the more difficult when they truly love us and want what is best for us. They can hinder our freedom, that personal center one must guard for oneself and the Holy Spirit. This is why, for instance, there are strict canons in Church law to verify the freedom of the person from the influence of others at the moment of lifelong commitment, be it marriage, religious vows, or Holy Orders. In Christ, the person has an absolute dignity. There is a story of love in your heart that is unique and personal, between yourself and God. No one can choose your lifetime commitment for you.

The problem may be in your own heart, however, and not in the words of your loved ones. You may be hiding in the security of what your parents want for you as a way of avoiding the commitment to which you feel called or out of fear of letting them down, hurting their feelings, or simply leaving their nest. This is yet another way to relinquish our precious freedom.

How many devout parents have pushed their sons to become priests which, in the end, has resulted in unnecessary struggles and unhappiness. How many young women have married the "Mr. Right" their parents or their BFFs had in mind for them! If you look too hard for the Lord to speak through others, those who say that they "see you making a good priest" and such, you might fail to hear the whisper of the Holy Spirit to your own heart.

On the same note, and even more seriously, an authentic spiritual director is one who leaves full liberty to the person, putting no pressure in one direction or another. He or she listens and accompanies the person, leaving room for the Spirit to speak. You should always feel complete freedom to continue with your spiritual director or not. Whether intentionally or unintentionally, a spiritual director can impose a spiritual weight that can be blinding or can lead to scruples. One can also feel tempted to try to please one's spiritual director, seeking the decision that will make him or her happy. That misses the whole point!

A relationship of spiritual fatherhood or motherhood is sometimes important for our growth, but it is not the same thing as the spiritual direction that is required for discernment. Spiritual fatherhood carries with it all the same issues as in family relations, and often in a more subtle way. The pressure from a familial, social, or spiritual relationship can become interiorized and buried in the heart of the young person who is discerning. A young adult might want to enter a certain religious order because it is the most prestigious, the most intellectual, or because it seems to have the right image. In many cultures, priesthood and religious life carries a social, material, and intellectual status, and so one enters not to give of oneself, but to receive.

Similarly, one might marry someone for money, popularity, or social status, more than out of love. Here, the story of St. Bernadette Soubirous' parents is touching. Her father could have married her mother's older sister and had her inheritance; instead, he married the woman he loved, the younger one who had almost no dowry. They got married out of love, against social norms, and in the face of a poor social structure that eventually led to their family being destitute and hungry, but also fertile soil for sanctity.

The influence of your friends and family can also make you flee from their idea of what is best for you. You might move towards a vocation in reaction against a father, a mother, a sibling, or even a coach, a teacher, a priest, etc. If they were too traditional or too authoritative, you might be tempted to flee commitment. If they were too permissive or worldly, you might be biased towards a more strict and radical religious call.

There are more subtle cases, too, such as a young woman who feels guilty in the wake of her parents' divorce, and in order to pay back this "debt," seeks religious life. These reactive movements of the heart often happen because of a resentment that is buried deep below the surface. Often, the person is not aware of those motivations. Time in prayer and spiritual direction help us realize whether feelings and motives are underpinned by wounds or by authentic desires inspired by the Holy Spirit.

Let us remember once again the one real motivation of a call, namely seeking where you will be better able to give of yourself, to love, to become holy. In the end, this is the only real question. This is also the condition for your happiness. All other motives – social, material, professional, family-related, emotional – will not fulfill your desire for happiness.

The aim of discernment is to help us overcome these influences, positive or negative, in order to arrive at true freedom and in order to find that path that will be a lasting source of happiness and support. The important choices in life must be as free as possible. This whole-hearted freedom is a requirement for the validity of a vow, but it is also a dimension of the grandeur of human dignity and of Christian personhood.

It is important to conduct your discernment with reverent discretion, to guard your heart, and to not blab about it casually to just anyone. The secret of your heart belongs to the King. Hopefully, your choice will lead to a blessing for your loved ones and for your relationship with them. But if this blessing is to be deep and lasting, it must be based upon a discernment that truly belongs to you, to that free sanctuary where you are yourself and where the Holy Spirit has His dwelling (*Catechism of the Catholic Church* 2563).

IV

Letting the Discernment
Take on Flesh

Taking a step is salvific.

Antoine de Saint Exupéry

1. Where are You Calling Me, Lord?

To wrap up the discernment, you need to ask of the Lord not only who and what you are called to be, but also where. Do not hesitate to ask kindly but "firmly" for God to grant you the happiness you hope for. This seems obvious. God is benevolent, and He knows your heart. But often, with a spirit of timidity, unworthiness, and fear, we do not dare to ask.

If you are in love, you must one day declare your love. The same with God. You might pray, for example, "My God, the desire of my heart is to serve you as a priest, as a religious, as a father or mother… if this is the happiness you intend for me, show me where you want me to serve." Do not be afraid of Christ. He is unsurpassable in generosity, kindness and tenderness. When He calls, He forces nothing. Rather, He grants all. You must ask Him, though, so that He may show you where He wants you to pave a road to holiness together with Him. You must ask in a solemn way – freely, soberly and prayerfully. You might even want to write it out or say it aloud, in order to articulate clearly what you seek.

You do not need to repeat this act over and over – God will have heard the first time. If He fails to get back to you right away, it is because the chosen time has not yet come. Be patient; be at peace.

2. Cross the Threshold

• *Courting Consecrated Life*

Is it time to take the next step? For those discerning religious life, if you have been in touch with a priest or a community, you may already have the right door open to you. If you feel called to diocesan life, your diocese has a vocations office ready to answer your call and offer you an interview. Some dioceses have discernment groups, retreats, and even a first year of formation, a "spirituality year," where you can plunge into a deeper time of discernment leading up to the rigors of intellectual, human, and pastoral formation that seminary life provides.

If you feel called to a religious community, ask if it is possible to spend a week or more living their life. Find the place where you feel at home – in consecrated life, your religious brothers or sisters will be like your family. For those interested in a missionary order, many communities might even send you abroad for a summer or a year. There are also a few such programs today that offer help for discernment "in general," not necessarily ordered towards their own community. They offer a time of mission that involves an intense life of community, prayer, and tools for discernment[7]. In vocational discernment, the goal is to receive a lifelong mission. In religious life, your community will first of all form your heart – your prayer life, lifestyle, and way of life. For this reason, apostolate will often have to wait for a few years. You will be formed, however, not

---

[7] See APPENDIX.

just to do service and evangelization, but to *be* a sign of the Kingdom, a permanent sign, and to let any service or works of the Gospel be the cup overflowing for the rest of your life. In the same way, diocesan seminaries are focusing more and more, at least in the beginning years, on spirituality, brotherhood, and healthy human growth. They are conscious that the pressure of studies or the thrill of an apostolate needs to be tempered in order to lay a foundation for a lifelong mission.

The heart, mind, and body are particularly ripe for such intense formation from about age 19 to 25. In these years, we establish values, habits, and a world-view that will last for life. This is why it is crucial to find the right conditions for discernment precisely during these years, and why so many religious orders do not accept new candidates over 30 or 35.

Unfortunately, college campuses are not always the most conducive to spiritual growth and formation. You must find a way to go against the flow of busyness, stress, pressure into a career path, competition to have the best image and reputation, etc. It is important not to become enticed by the glorified freedom of no commitments and boundaries, nor the vices of drinking, pornography, and a certain independence that isolates students and leaves many feeling lonely.

• *Courting your Sweetheart*

Guys, if you are in love, walk across the gym and ask her to dance! Ladies, show him that you are interested! It is good to get to know this person as a friend, especially within a group of friends. Sooner or later, though, you need to ask them on a date. You also need to come before the Lord together, to feel what it is like to pray together.

When the time comes, you can receive that gift that the Church provides, in her wisdom: engagement. What a beautiful time to grow. Know that the Church canonically requires six months of marriage preparation, and many dioceses in America require eight months or even a year. This is from the time you first begin to meet with a priest or lay minister, not from the time you propose. Remember, then, that you can begin this marriage prep even before your official engagement, if you can find a priest or marriage prep ministry that is willing. This way, you can have the time and freedom to use the tools the Church provides for discerning a relationship.

Thus, when you do get engaged, another way to place your hopes in the light of the Lord is to summon the support of the Church, and to let your love be lifted up as a witness by having your engagement blessed, even within a Mass. Priests have ritual books with these options spelled out.

These steps of engagement are not aimed at sealing a covenant, but rather helping you enter into an openness to the Spirit – an openness towards deeper understanding and strength, but also the openness to discerning whether this is truly your call. Inevitably, it will be a discovery of the imperfections hidden in your fiancé, in yourself, and in your relationship.

Let the illusions fall, and realize that the "perfect" man or woman, or the "perfect" human love does not exist, at least not the way you may have imagined. Life isn't a Hollywood movie! Instead, entering into a covenant, by marriage, religious vows, or Holy Orders, means embracing the perfection of the

Kingdom of Heaven. We can accept and adhere to a lifelong commitment, with all its variables, precisely because it is an act of faith in Jesus Christ, true God and true Man. His fullness awaits us in Heaven, and the experience of beauty and love we have here below is only a foretaste.

Celibacy for the Kingdom is the essential call of consecrated life. The consecrated person embraces the fullness of the eternal mystical Wedding Feast, a foretaste of the life of the world to come. However, married couples also need to understand their covenant as a sign of Heaven. Their faithfulness expresses the faithfulness of God's love which never changes, always forgives, and is always life-giving.

With this eternal perspective, as St. Paul tells us, the sufferings of this life are nothing in comparison to the glory that awaits us (Romans 8:18). In this light of eternity, we indeed find meaning and peace for the task, the unique place that the Lord prepares for us in this present life. As a young woman aspiring to her Carmelite call, Blessed Elizabeth of the Trinity said, "In the light of eternity, life is really something serious."

3. If it didn't Work Out... No Regrets, at Least Now You Know!

Good news! Even if you had all the right conditions, followed all the criteria outlined in this book, and avoided all the pitfalls, you still have the right to get it wrong. You even have the right for all this discernment to take years.

The road to the priesthood takes at least six years. Less than half of the seminarians who enter are ever ordained. They leave for various reasons, and there is nothing out of the ordinary or shameful about it. These are years given to the Lord, marvelous years that make a young man just as ready to be a good husband. If you are called to religious life, many big steps lie between the day you enter and the morning of your final vows: candidacy, postulancy, novitiate, temporary vows... Each one of these stages take time, leaving room for freedom and the possibility to reconsider the call, with a chance to leave if your discernment has not found peace and confirmation. It is not time lost. Every year spent dedicated to the Lord is a gain, and will bear fruit in your life, wherever your path leads you.

In the same way, for marriage, many couples pass through a time of dating, and then possibly even a "dating fast," before entering into the time of serious courting and engagement. If you got it wrong despite two years of prayer and prudence, at least now you know that this was not the person or the vocation you are called to. Had you never crossed the threshold, you may have regretted it all your life.

A woman once shared that she felt a call to religious life two months before her wedding. She told God "no," and for years, she carried this regret, despite her happy marriage and children. Obviously, she needed to put the past behind her and welcome with her whole heart the beautiful family God had granted her. God blesses your choice, your covenant once you have made it. But before we make that choice, we need to be bold enough to listen and to take steps.

One of today's idols is security or control. People would like to be able to stop, go in slow motion, or even rewind their lives to make sure life follows the plot they have in mind. The movie *Click* illustrates how quick we are to shop for that remote control that can make us masters of our destiny. Michael (Adam Sandler), after using a special remote control to fast forward through some dull or unpleasant moments of his life, ends up realizing that even the tough strokes in life are part of its ultimate goodness.

Taking risks means daring to "get it wrong," but the only avenue of true love involves risk. It is better not to find yourself lamenting one day, "If only I had asked Juliet's hand," or "If only I had the courage to ask to enter that community." So many not-so-young adults keep dreaming their destiny or their past because they lacked the courage to give the Lord a year to explore and verify a vocation. Those who did take the concrete steps across that threshold come out on the other side feeling much more free, even if the story did not turn out as they had foreseen.

4. When you finally found what you're looking for

If you trust the Lord with all your heart and try to follow the advice given in this book step-by-step, God will show you what path of holiness He has planned for you. It may not happen overnight, but it will happen. The reason for this is not that this book is infallible, of course (so much more could be said!); rather, it is because of the faithfulness of God. In 2 Chronicles 16:9 it is written that "the Lord's eyes rove to and fro across the whole world to support those whose hearts are loyal to him." That's you! In the Gospels, Jesus is saddened when so many people fail to seek Heaven with all their hearts. Strive to keep your heart open to God, depending ever more on your Heavenly Father, and He'll take care of you, day after day. It can take longer than you had hoped: be patient! It is the story of your life that God is writing page after page, and it is a story of holiness. When you do discover your call, rejoice and be glad! Thank God for this precious gift that He has given you. Like the parables in the Gospel, sell all that you have to buy this field filled with treasure; contemplate the value of this pearl of great price with a heart full of gratitude. Whether you find yourself deeply in love with a spouse, fulfilled in a religious community or as a priest, or wake up every morning excited to live your dream, offer each moment to the Lord. In happiness and in trial, implore the Lord for the grace you need to be faithful to your call. This is in no way the end of your journey, but rather the beginning of the next chapter!

Conclusion

Life in Abundance!

To fall in love with God is the greatest romance;
to seek Him, the greatest adventure;
to find Him, the greatest human achievement.

St. Augustine

Writing about two hundred years before the time of Jesus, the wise man Sirach penned these words, "My child, when you come to serve the Lord, prepare yourself for trials. Be sincere of heart and steadfast, and do not be impetuous in time of adversity. Cling to him, do not leave him, that you may prosper in your last days" (Sirach 2:1-3). The same holds true today. If you decide to respond to a particular call in your heart to serve the Lord as a priest or religious, arm yourself with courage. You have chosen a challenging path. The climb can be steep, and many around you may not follow you on this path. You will be a sign of contradiction for many, even a scandal. What is more, it is a narrow path where you can only pass through single file. Just like a mountain, though, it will take you to marvelous vistas. You will never be alone.

Do not think that marriage will be easier or less heroic. As a couple, you must become holy; all the more so once the little ones arrive. Don't worry! There will be plenty of opportunities to grow in love. In any case (priest, religious, couples or singles), the goal is the same: holiness! The author Georges Bernanos wrote, "Holiness, this is the sole adventure!" Christ awaits you. Do not wait for Heaven in order to be with Him and to taste the infinite love of the Father. On this point, let us be impatient – eternal life has already begun!

Appendix

Discernment Year:
A few examples

A few examples, to make it practical: a couple of discernment places are *Heart's Home* in New York (www.usa.heartshome. org), *NET Team* based in St. Paul, MN (www.netusa.org), and *Christ in the City* in Denver, CO (www.christinthecitymis-sionaries.com). FOCUS is a program whose formation encourages discernment, although it involves a two-year commitment (www.focus.org). An intellectual program, like the *Augustine Institute*, also equips students to serve the Church and grow in holiness, on a two-year degree program, whatever their vocation (www.augustineinstitute.org). These programs provide an excellent opportunity to serve the Lord and grow in spiritual maturity with other like-minded people. They can be a real help in discernment, although it is important to keep in mind the pitfalls mentioned concerning short-term goals, and should not be used to escape deeper questions.

At the Community of the Beatitudes, we continue to offer a program that is called *School of Life*. Whether through a time in the Denver house or trips to Europe, Israel and beyond, the goal is an immersion in the nuts and bolts of a vocation in the Church: moving as a religious community every day through a rhythm of Mass, Adoration, Missions and Apostolate, Evangelization, Liturgy of the Hours, meals, dishes, and manual work. The *rhythms* of daily and weekly life with spiritual direction and a few teachings, along with high times of praise, celebration, and recreation on the weekends. Community life provides an environment to go beyond the surface level, challenging you to address the tougher issues and deeper consolations, but in an environment of fraternal charity and ecclesial guidance. What is more, both celibate and the married vocations are present in the Community of the Beatitudes, held up in their respective dignity and complimentary gifts at the heart of the Church (*School of Life* info on www.beatitudes.us).